Life's Challenges

WEEKENDS WITH DAD

What to Expect When Your Parents Divorce

by Melissa Higgins

illustrated by Wednesday Kirwan

PICTURE WINDOW BOOKS
a capstone imprint

Saturday mornings were always super-loud at our house.
The morning Mom and Dad told us their big news, though,
it was quiet. That's how I knew something was wrong.

I thought my sister, Sam, and I were in trouble.

Mom and Dad sat us down in the living room. Mom said she and Dad had some problems. They had tried to work them out but couldn't. She said they loved Sam and me very much. But they weren't in love with each other anymore.

One out of four kids in the United States lives with one parent.

"Mom and I will always be your mom and dad," Dad said.
"But we're separating. We need some time apart."

Dad was moving to his own apartment.
Sam and I would live with Mom for now.

My heart pounded. I felt hot and cold at the same time. Why was Dad moving away?

Then I remembered. Last week Mom had gotten mad when she saw the new soccer cleats Dad had bought me. She and Dad had a huge fight over money. So it *was* my fault!

"You can return the shoes!" I shouted. **"I don't need them!"**

6

That's when Mom gave me a big hug. She said I hadn't done anything wrong. This was a grown-up problem.

Dad hugged me too.

Not too long after lunchtime, he was gone. I'd never felt so sad.

When parents are fighting a lot, some kids feel relieved when their parents separate and the fighting stops. It's OK to feel relieved, scared, sad, or angry. Everyone feels things differently.

Monday morning, Mrs. Niles went over our spelling words. All I could think about was Mom and Dad getting back together. Perry, my best friend, asked me what was wrong. I just shrugged. I couldn't tell him. I didn't want to talk to anybody.

Why hadn't Mom and Dad tried harder to fix their problems? Moms and dads can fix anything! Would Dad be OK by himself? Would Mom move away too? *Then* what would happen to Sam and me?

Why couldn't this happen to some other kid?

Some kids feel jealous of friends whose parents are still together. It may help to remember that even kids with married parents don't have perfect lives.

Mrs. Niles knew about the separation. Mom had called her. A couple days later, Mrs. Niles helped me join a group of other kids at school. Their moms and dads had split up too. I didn't know there were so many of us! It felt good to know I wasn't alone.

We get together every Wednesday. The other kids understand what I'm feeling.

We usually sit on the floor in a big circle and talk about stuff. One thing I learned: It's not good to keep feelings bottled up.

Our school counselor, Miss Sanchez, is really nice. After we're all done talking, she lets us play games and hang out for a while.

I've learned a lot from the group. When I feel sad or angry, I kick my soccer ball.

When I don't understand something, I ask my mom or dad questions.

I call Dad when I miss him.

When I just need to talk,
I go to Mrs. Niles or Perry.
They're both great listeners.

About a month after Dad moved out, Mom said she and Dad were getting a divorce. That meant they were splitting up for good. I kind of knew it was coming, but I still cried. Mom said she and Dad had to go to court. They had to figure out child support and who would take care of my sister and me most of the time.

A woman from the court even talked to me. She asked a lot of questions, like where I wanted to live. I didn't want to hurt anyone's feelings. But she told me to be honest. I liked having a say.

It's weird living in two places. Sam and I share a room at Dad's but not at Mom's. We have a set of clothes and toys in both places. There's a big visitation calendar at both places too. The calendars remind us when we're supposed to be at which place.

Our first morning at Dad's, Sam said, **"That's not how Mom makes pancakes."**

I thought the same thing, but I shushed Sam anyway. I didn't want Dad to get upset.

The way things go at Dad's house may be different from the way things go at Mom's. It's OK to feel confused at first.

17

But Dad said it was OK. He wanted us to tell him when something bothered us. **"I'll always love you two,"** he said. **"No matter what."** Then he asked us to help him fix the pancakes.

Sam and I had fun helping. We made smiley faces with chocolate chips. Dad poured loops of blueberry syrup for hair. The pancakes were the best ever.

After a divorce, you may feel like you need to grow up fast. But being a kid is your only job.

It's been a year now since Mom and Dad divorced. They both come to my games when they can. I still wish we lived together in one house. But I'm getting used it.

What's not so cool is that when I'm with Dad, I miss Mom. When I'm with Mom, I miss Dad. Sometimes I feel like I'm living in two different worlds.

But Mom and Dad pay attention to me. And they're usually nice to each other. That really helps, because I love them both—a lot.

Just because we don't all live together anymore doesn't mean Mom and Dad love me any less. Their love for me and Sam is forever.

Read More

Brown, Laurene Krasny, and Marc Brown. *Dinosaurs Divorce*. Boston: Atlantic Monthly Press, 1986.

Gray, Kes. *Mom and Dad Glue*. Hauppauge, N.Y.: Barron's, 2009.

Levins, Sandra. *Was It the Chocolate Pudding? A Story for Little Kids About Divorce*. Washington, D.C.: Magination Press, 2005.

Schmitz, Tamara. *Standing on My Own Two Feet: A Child's Affirmation of Love in the Midst of Divorce*. New York: Price Stern Sloan, 2008.

Internet Sites

FactHound offers a safe, fun way to find Internet sites related to this book. All of the sites on FactHound have been researched by our staff.

Here's all you do:

Visit *www.facthound.com*

Type in this code: 9781404866782

Super-cool stuff! Check out projects, games and lots more at **www.capstonekids.com**

Glossary

child support—payments made to help with children's living expenses

court—a place where legal decisions are made

divorce—the legal steps ending a marriage

separate—to choose to no longer live together

visitation—the time separated or divorced parents spend with their kids

Index

Look for all the books in
the Life's Challenges series:

Good-bye, Jeepers

The Night Dad Went to Jail

Saying Good-bye to Uncle Joe

Weekends with Dad

Thanks to our advisers for their expertise, research, and advice:

Michele Goyette-Ewing, PhD
Director of Psychology Training
Yale Child Study Center

Terry Flaherty, PhD
Professor of English
Minnesota State University, Mankato

Editor: Jill Kalz
Designer: Alison Thiele
Art Director: Nathan Gassman
Production Specialist: Sarah Bennett
The illustrations in this book were created with gouache and colored pencil.

Picture Window Books
1710 Roe Crest Drive
North Mankato, MN 56003
877-845-8392
www.capstonepub.com

All books published by Picture Window Books
are manufactured with paper containing at least
10 percent post-consumer waste.

Library of Congress Cataloging-in-Publication Data
Higgins, Melissa, 1953–
  Weekends with Dad : what to expect when your parents divorce /
by Melissa Higgins ; illustrated by Wednesday Kirwan.
    p. cm. — (Life's challenges)
  ISBN 978-1-4048-6678-2 (library binding)
  1. Children of divorced parents—Juvenile literature. 2.
Divorce—Juvenile literature. I. Kirwan, Wednesday. II. Title.
  HQ777.5.H54 2012
  306.89—dc22
                                    2011007458

Printed in the United States of America in North Mankato, Minnesota.
112011   006464R

3/12